The Bonsai Theory of Church Growth

KEN HEMPHILL

THE BONSAI THEORY

OF CHURCH GROWTH

BROADMAN PRESS
NASHVILLE, TENNESSEE

© Copyright 1991 • Broadman Press

All rights reserved

4260-45

ISBN: 0-8054-6045-4

Dewey Decimal Classification: 254.5

Subject Heading: CHURCH GROWTH

Library of Congress Card Catalog Number

Printed in the United States of America

Inside illustrations by Leland Howe.

To Carl and Ruby Hemphill
Recently retired from forty-seven years
of active local church ministry—
Parents who taught me to love the Lord
and His Bride, the church

CONTENTS

INTRODUCTION

A Passion for Bonsai

A few years ago I developed a passion for bonsai trees. Bonsai are nothing more than miniature versions of real trees. I'm not sure what spurred my interest. Perhaps it's somewhat genetic. My dad has always been interested in all sorts of plants. Even though he lives in North Carolina he grows pineapples, oranges, coffee trees, and other assorted tropical and traditional plants. Truthfully, I never exhibited a real interest or knack for plants while under my dad's roof. Maybe this sort of genetic input takes time to mature. I guess it was a latent recessive gene.

Looking back, the movie *The Karate Kid* may have been the stimulus that kicked my "growing-plants-gene" out of neutral and into drive. My middle daughter, Rachael, was taking karate lessons at the time and we saw the film together. While she was impressed with the karate kicks and punches, I was fascinated by the miniature trees. They looked just like the real thing, only much, much smaller.

Not long after that movie I was on my *annual* family shopping trip to the mall. Malls are not my thing, and shopping is certainly not a favorite pastime for me. I dutifully trudged into and out of various clothing and toy stores according to the age of whichever daughter had me in tow. I was at the point of physical and financial exhaustion when I spotted a live bonsai. Actually I discovered a table full of bonsai trees.

I was fascinated by the tiny trees before me. They *looked* like real trees! They *were* real trees! I began to inquire concerning their care and feeding, and, ah yes, price. The girls soon became bored with my shopping interest. They were quickly dispatched to nearby stores to browse while I continued to inspect tree after tree. Finally, after much deliberation, I bought a small pine tree in a shallow blue pot. Little did I suspect that this decorative shallow pot was one of the keys to the mystery of the bonsai.

I took my first tree to my office at church. I placed it in a window with just the proper amount of sunlight. I watered it dutifully per the instructions on the little attached card on the "care and feeding of bonsai." All appeared to go well for the first several months. But alas after these initial successful months my bonsai began to drop needles and to show all the apparent signs of a sickness unto death. My diagnosis proved accurate and my thirty-dollar tree perished.

I was convinced that my secretary was the culprit in the ultimately demise of my treasured tree. No doubt she had failed to water it faithfully while I was out of the office for a prolonged speaking engagement. You see, a bonsai requires daily watering since the root structure is so very small. The tiny, helpless victim was summarily pitched out without even a decent burial.

It wasn't long, however, until I acquired my next bonsai. My secretaries gave this one to me, proving my theory of neglect. A guilt gift, no doubt! This bonsai was accompanied by a fairly large pamphlet containing directions for growing a bonsai. Why should I bother with reading such obvious trivia? How hard could it be to keep a tree small and alive at the same time? I tossed my book into a drawer.

My new tree flourished for a while, but then it too began to look sickly. Then I made a brilliant and well-calculated move. I read the bonsai pamphlet! If all else fails, read the instructions! I found this book fascinating. I soon bought another and then another bonsai book. When we traveled, I looked for bonsai at nurseries or in collections. With the aid of my trusty manuals I soon began a collection of bonsai trees. Some I bought, others I started from small seedlings. I now have more than a dozen trees in my collection. I have a tiny tangerine that bears real fruit, several flowering trees, three different kinds of pines, and even a few hardwoods. These trees require a great deal of attention, but their miniature beauty never ceases to amaze me and visitors to our home.

This past summer two young ladies who were serving as summer interns at our church stayed in our home. One afternoon they sat watching me as I meticulously cared for my prized bonsai. They were astounded when I pulled one tree from its container, shook the dirt from the root ball, uncurled the roots, and began cutting them off.

"What are you doing," they shrieked. "You'll kill it!"

Typical reaction of a novice! I assured them that I was not killing the tree, I was only making sure that it would remain small. This peaked their interest.

"What else do you do to keep them small?"

I explained to them in great detail the secret behind the bonsai. The small pot, pruning the roots, and pinching back new growth were all critical to keeping the bonsai small and healthy. You can sound reasonably brilliant if you read the instructions!

Bonsai Churches

As we discussed the art of the bonsai, *it dawned on me that the principles that keep a tree small will also keep a church small.* I know it sounds funny, but it's true. Most pastors and laymen that I talk to want their church to grow. They want to reach their community for Christ. Despite their desire to grow, their church remains the same size. *Why,* they wonder, *are we not growing?*

It is, in fact, the nature of a living organism to grow. All the biblical images of the church such as the body, the field, and the building presuppose a natural process of growth. It is my conviction that many churches, without knowing it, are doing things which virtually assure that they will remain small—a sort of bonsai church. If we can remove the actions that inhibit natural growth, the church should grow in a natural and proportionate manner.

It should be recognized from the beginning, that as there are numerous sizes of trees, there will be many sizes of churches. The giant redwood is not intrinsically better than the diminutive dogwood. Each tree is different, each having its own form, function, and beauty. This book is not about megachurches. It does not presuppose that all churches should or could become very large churches. It does, however, suggest that a church, as a living organism, should grow to its natural, God-given size. When Jesus established the church, as recorded in Matthew 16, He promised *He would build His church.* Thus we can say that church growth is at once natural and supernatural. It is *supernatural* because God gives the growth and it is *natural* because the church was created as a living body to grow. The church must grow in such a manner that it fulfills the Great Commission in its own community. I have come to believe that church growth is natural and that artificial measures must be taken to keep a church from growing.

Are You Creating a Bonsai Church?

1
KEEP THE POT SMALL

The bonsai pot may be the most identifiable accessory for the growing of bonsai trees. The pots come in numerous shapes and sizes. Some are very shallow, designed for planting a bonsai forest (several trees grouped together). Others are tall and somewhat narrow, used primarily for trees that cascade downward. Many look simply like miniature versions of more familiar flowerpots. Most are ornate ceramic pots containing Oriental-looking scenes and beautiful glazes. All of them are expensive when you consider their relative size. You would think that you wouldn't have to pay so dearly for such a small hunk of clay.

After only a cursory reading of my collection of bonsai books, I discovered that fitting the right pot to the right tree was an integral part of the act of growing bonsai. The bonsai grower must take into account factors such as the size, shape, and color of the tree when making this crucial decision. In my case I must add a fourth criteria—price. Once the pot and the plant have been chosen, you're ready to go to work. The small tree must be placed in just the right position in the pot for the proper aesthetic beauty. Once this task has been completed you have embarked on your bonsai journey.

Yet the pot is much more than a simple decorative holder for a little tree. The pot in many ways helps to determine the size of the tree. The beautiful glazed dish must hold the dirt and roots that will support the tree's healthy growth. One of the secrets to the small size of the bonsai is the limited space for root growth.

This discovery about little trees applies to churches as well. The size of the container in which a congregation is planted will in many ways determine the size it will grow to in maturity. Like the bonsai container there are several dimensions to the church container.

The Building

The most obvious container for the church is its building, its physical plant. Notice that the church and the building are not one and the same. The church is made up of people. It is a living, growing organism. The building is made of bricks, mortar, wood, and steel. It functions simply as a container for the church. The container can either restrict or facilitate growth.

It took years of reading and practical experience before I could accept the fact that when any portion of the building is 80 percent filled, the church's natural growth will be inhibited and finally stopped. This rule of thumb can be applied to the worship center, an individual classroom, or the educational facility as a whole. Many churches have limited their growth because their facility restricts natural growth and development. Just as the container size affects the root ball of a bonsai so the facility can restrict church growth. A church can be committed to growth, doing outreach, organizing people in small groups, and all the other right things and still not grow because the pot is too small.

Some church leaders overlook this principle because they walk down the hallways and observe that they could put four more chairs in this room and three more in this one and so forth. A class or small group may actually overcrowd a particular room for a single high-attendance emphasis, but they will not consistently maintain this full status. If a room will accommodate twenty adults, the class occupying that room will have about sixteen persons in regular attendance. The class may continue to enroll new persons, but the average attendance will remain static. The small-pot syndrome has had its effect.

This limiting factor is more pronounced but often ignored in preschool or children's rooms. Preschoolers and children require more floor space by the very nature of their educational needs. A particular church may have available rooms for new adult classes, but their preschool rooms are already overcrowded. Here once again the small-pot theory stifles the ability of this church to grow. If the preschool division or another similar division is unable to expand, the entire church's ability to grow will be restricted.

In our rapid growth years at First Baptist, Norfolk, I often thought we could grow a big tree in a small pot. When I looked at the tremendous growth, it often appeared that we had defied this principle of church growth. Suddenly, Sunday School growth stopped at an average of 1,700 persons in attendance. We continued to grow in worship because we had just completed an addition to our worship center, and we had room to expand. We already had two Sunday Schools and two worship services, but Sunday School growth was static.

Upon close examination we discovered we had no rooms in which to create *new* small groups. It is a basic truth that new groups grow more quickly. Thus our ability to grow had been limited by our container. We decided to begin a third Sunday School. About two hundred persons understood our dilemma and made the move to the early Sunday School. In a matter of months our Sunday School surged to over 1,900 in attendance. By enlarging our space we were able to accommodate new growth. A small pot artificially limits a tree from growing to its natural size. A small building can limit a church from growing to the natural size for its community.

Many church families resign themselves to the small pot because they can't afford to build or land is not readily available. You can increase the size of your pot without building. Consider off-site small groups. If there is a school or office building nearby, you can rent or borrow space. We have had several singles classes who have met over the years in conference rooms at nearby hospitals and motels and in a restaurant. Interestingly, some people attended these off-site classes who might never have come to the church building. You can also employ multiple Sunday Schools. This is one of the least expensive methods of enlarging your container. The building is already available and the costs of the additional heating/cooling and lights is very small. When you use multiple Sunday Schools you will not have 100 percent more room because some groups such as preschool and younger children use the same space for the entire Sunday School and worship period. You can usually count on approximately a 70 percent increase in real space. Multiple Sunday Schools and worship services provide many advantages and should be considered for both a short-term and a long-term pot enlargement idea. I know this sounds like hard work. It is, but it's worth the effort when we consider the outreach potential created by new space.

If you continue to reach your community, you *will* need to build additional space. This should be seen as a joy and not as a necessary burden of church growth. The construction of buildings for the purpose of evangelistic outreach often serves to stimulate even more growth. The community interprets this as a sign of life. The people will see it as a commitment to fulfill the Great Commission.

However you choose to enlarge the container, enlarge it you must if you want to remove an artificial restriction to natural growth.

The Land

The acreage available to the church family is another form of container. The church building and parking space must match the acreage. A good rule of thumb is that each acre will accommodate 100 people. If people have nowhere to park, you limit the number who will attend your church. I often encounter pious unbelievers at this point. "If people really want to come to church they would be willing to walk!" That sounds good, but often those loudest in singing that refrain would themselves be unwilling to walk several blocks to church. Some mature believers who understand the mission of the church will be willing to walk a distance to church, but the unsaved persons that the Great Commission church is attempting to reach won't walk across the street to visit your church.

You must provide adequate parking. Our church has experienced and continues to experience problems with the parking lot. We do not have sufficient parking. It has been a restriction to our growth. Were it not for a good number of folk who park away from our church property, our growth would have stopped years ago.

A few years ago we instituted a preferred parking program. What, you might ask, is preferred parking? Let me illustrate by telling you where I got the idea. When I was being recruited to play football for a college team, I attended a game with an alumnus. Near the stadium a guard spied a sticker on his car and waved him through the waiting traffic and parked him next to the gate right at the fifty-yard line. That was my first experience with *preferred parking*.

It has been my experience that in the Christian life things are often opposite that of the world's standard. The first shall be last! The leader is the servant! Thus our preferred parking is off our church property. We took our cue from Romans 12:10, "Giving preference to one another in honor." We ask Christians to give up their space near the church in preference to those who need the on-site spaces—the elderly, the handicapped, parents with small children, and the unsaved who are looking for a good excuse not to come to church.

The first priority would be to provide adequate on-site parking for expanded growth. If you cannot, you must use off-site parking. To reach newcomers, and particularly the unsaved, you should reserve the premium spaces for visitors. Well-marked and easily accessible visitor places are essential for the church committed to reaching its community.

The Organization Pot

While the building and the land may be the most obvious containers, they are not the *only* pots that can restrict growth. Your organization itself can restrict growth. If the organization of the church remains small, the ultimate size of the church will match the organization size. For example, if you have four adult classes each averaging twelve persons, you will not grow appreciably from this figure of forty-eight adults in attendance until you enlarge the organization. You must add another class or, better, two classes. The organization of the church is somewhat like the root system of a tree. If the organization remains small, the resulting tree will reflect the size of the organization.

Many churches have practiced this principle of church growth through expanding the organization without realizing it. Let's take a church that has been averaging about one hundred in Sunday School for years. One day two young married couples come to the pastor and ask if they can start a new class for young couples. The class is started with the two couples who quickly invite other couples in the community who were not previously attending church. At the end of the year the pastor notices that the average attendance is now 112. What happened? The organization was expanded and growth followed.

You may be wondering, *What is the ideal size for an adult small group unit or Sunday School class?* Most church growth experts point to *attendance* figures ranging from twelve to fifteen with an *enrollment* of twenty-five to thirty. Some unique situations enable classes to grow beyond this size, but the crucial factor is the organizational structure of the class for ministry. When a class becomes too large, it often fails to care adequately for the relational needs of its members.

Churches may have high-attendance Sundays or special events and greatly improve attendance for a short time. However, attendance gradually drops back to its *normal level* unless the organization itself is expanded to provide for a larger tree. This organization pot cannot be overlooked if you desire to reach your community for Christ.

The Leadership Pot

The organization itself cannot be enlarged unless the leadership pool is enlarged. The growing church must have sufficient numbers of well-trained and committed leaders if it is to continue to grow in a natural and healthy fashion. Some people believe that this is actually the key principle of church growth. It is certainly critical. Little can be done to expand the organization without sufficient leadership to staff the enlarged organization.

Many churches overlook this principle by not providing for sufficient professional staff members. The professional staff is responsible for equipping the saints for the work of ministry. Most church-growth leaders recommend one professional staff person per 150 to 200 people in Sunday School. If the leadership structure breaks down at this most basic level, little can be accomplished in recruiting and training sufficient lay leadership. The church committed to growth will have to ensure that the leadership pot is continually enlarged.

We must plan ahead and provide sufficient budget to call staff persons. Often a growing church will need to call an individual who will share two responsibilities such as music and youth, youth and education, or some other combination. This may be wise during these early growth years. Every staff person will have multiple tasks. As the church grows, greater specialization is preferable. Most staff persons who are in a combination position are stronger in one area than the other. Allow them to serve in that area and bring someone else on board to do the other task. All of your staff should be involved in evangelistic outreach whatever their job description. A primary function of the professional ministerial staff is to equip the laypersons for the work of ministry. A growing professional staff does not mean that fewer laypersons will be required. However, a growing staff does require a commitment on the part of the church to call and compensate sufficient staff for church growth.

If we are going to enlarge the leadership pot, a majority of staff time must be spent equipping lay leaders. This is the biblical picture painted by the apostle Paul in Ephesians 4:11-16. Every growing church will *always* face the need for more leadership. This need should never deter you from reaching your community for Christ.

At the end of Matthew 9, Jesus declared that the fields are ripe unto harvest. The limiting factor, Jesus pointed out, was the lack of laborers. Jesus then did two things. He exhorted the disciples to pray for sufficient laborers. Few churches spend adequate time praying for laborers before they actually seek them out. Prayer is the key to all church growth. The second thing Jesus did was to send His disciples on a missionary journey to seek lost folk. This is somewhat surprising! Many churches become paralyzed when they don't have sufficient leadership. They think, *Why should we do outreach? We can't care for the ones we have now*. They stop reaching out, and then they stop growing because they lose their focus on the Great Commission. This accounts for the thousands of churches that have grown and plateaued. Follow Jesus' example. Pray and reach out.

The Vision Pot

In many situations the most confining pot may be that of vision. Churches often fail to see and seize the opportunities for growth right in front of them. The early disciples were sometimes guilty of restricted vision. In John 4, Jesus instructed the disciples to lift up their eyes and look on the fields for they were ripe for the harvest. The disciples were unable to see this opportunity for growth. They were, at that moment, in Samaria. The long-standing animosity between the Jews and the Samaritans had restricted the vision of the disciples.

Small vision hampers church growth. A church may have small vision because of class or racial barriers like those of the disciples. They assume that the folk in the trailer park wouldn't feel comfortable here. In a similar manner we can ignore those who live in the so-called "better" sections of our community. We often fail to consider their needs. Vision can be limited by the lack of space, land, money, resources, or leadership. We can find ourselves in a never-ending cycle of negativity.

I have had the opportunity to share growth principles in conferences across the country. I find it fascinating that in almost every situation I hear pastors and laypersons decrying the fact that their location is the most difficult location for growing a church. It appears that everyone finds their soil unsuitable for church growth! Because of this lack of vision, many churches languish in a bonsai condition. In each of these locations I have also encountered pastors and people who see unlimited potential. In most cases someone else is growing a great church; therefore, they see that it *can* be done. In others, they see the absence of a great church as a golden opportunity. They exclaim, "No one is doing it here; the opportunities are absolutely unlimited." What a difference vision makes!

A church will never have sufficient resources for growth until it catches a great vision for reaching its community. The vision must come first. Many believers and churches fail to reach their full potential because they do not understand the crucial role of *vision*. Before the church will grow in a natural manner, there must be a thorough understanding of the biblical foundations of the church. Once we understand its *divine* potential, we will have unrestricted vision. As a starting point I would recommend careful study of *The Official Rulebook for the New Church Game*.[1]

The vision must begin in the heart of the pastor before it penetrates the church. Once the pastor catches God's vision for the church, he must boldly share it with the congregation. He must preach, teach, and encourage others to catch a glimpse of the supernatural empowering of the church. Once a majority of the leaders and members of the church catch a vision of the church unleashed, they will discover solutions for the problems that cause the church to struggle.

Jesus promised His disciples that *He would build* His church (Matt. 16:18). That's a supernatural promise that will not return void. You can, however, restrict that growth by a pot which artificially limits the natural process of supernatural church growth. "Where there is no vision, the people perish" (Prov. 29:18, KJV).

Fertile Thoughts and Actions

1. The building can limit your church's ability to grow. What is the maximum size of your Sunday School and worship facilities based upon the 80 percent full principle?

2. What possibilities are there for off-site Sunday School classes?

3. Do acreage and parking inhibit your church and Sunday School's growth? What can be done to expand your land and parking possibilities?

4. Effective organization is based upon the ability of the church to create new units. How many existing units in your Sunday School are over their maximum enrollment and attendance for maximum ministry? How many new units need to be started in order for your Sunday School to experience growth?

5. The ability of any Sunday School and church to grow largely depends upon its ability to enlist new leaders. There should be at

least one worker for every eight persons enrolled in Sunday School. What is the worker/member ratio in your Sunday School?

6. What is your vision for your Sunday School and church? Imagine what your Sunday School will look like three years from now. What do you see? How will it be different? How will you help these changes to occur?

7. What is your vision for your own personal growth as a Sunday School and church leader? Are you growing so that your Sunday School and church can continue to grow also? Develop an outline for your personal growth for the next year. What will you read? What conferences will you attend? Who will you invite to your church so that you and your church can hear from other growth experiences?

Note

1. Ken Hemphill, *The Official Rulebook for the New Church Game* (Nashville: Broadman Press, 1990).

Bonsai Theory of Growth

Size of Pot — Classrooms

                        80% rule

     Parking — 100/acre

Class size 12-15 (25-30 enrolled)
            regular attendance

2

PRUNE THE ROOTS

The most difficult bonsai technique for me to accept was the annual or biannual pruning of the roots. You heard right! On a regular basis you must remove the bonsai from its container, comb the dirt away from the root structure, and prune the roots. Because of the limited size of the bonsai container, the bonsai can easily become root-bound. The small size of the container limits the tree's ability to gather life-giving nutrients; therefore, it is essential that the roots be maintained at a suitable size for the container.

The first time I performed this task I knew I had killed my prized tree. Theoretically I understood that pruning the roots was essential if I was going to keep my tree small. I had one particularly beautiful bonsai with lovely white blooms. I had let it grow for

37

three years without pruning the roots. I began to notice an appreciable difference in the number of blooms on the tree. A friend, more established in the art of growing small trees, diagnosed the problem—root-bound—the roots must be cut back. I panicked! *I can't do it!*

With fear and trepidation I performed the mandatory root pruning with the tenderness of a surgeon. To my surprise my tree didn't die. It is, nonetheless, the most traumatic time in the life of the bonsai and its owner. The tree is placed at risk during the time of root pruning.

Yes, indeed, churches prune roots to keep themselves small. Often they do it without understanding that they are involved in root pruning or that this process will ensure that their church will remain small. Let's look at a few examples of how root pruning can produce a bonsai church!

Enrollment Pruning

Many churches go through an annual root pruning by lopping off members on the roll who have not attended during the last year. It is difficult to determine how this process came to be so prevalent in many churches. I suspect it came about because someone wanted to know what percentage of the membership attended on a particular Sunday. Many Bible study classes take great pride in having 100 percent of their enrollment in attendance. This is really not a difficult goal to accomplish. You need merely to trim off all those people who do not attend regularly.

I am concerned about those people on our church rolls who are inactive or sporadic at best. The best way to deal with these cumbersome *extra* roots, however, is not to cut them off, but to seek them out and restore them to fellowship. One often discovers that in pruning away what appears to be dead roots, healthy roots nearby are often damaged. Our primary goal is not to boast about the percentage of members present, but to reach the unsaved in our community and to care for those in our fellowship. We're not caring for anyone when we prune them from our rolls. We simply lose contact and opportunity for ministry. The church that goes through the annual process of root pruning will invariably remain small.

A few years ago I went to California to lead several Sunday School growth conferences. I arrived in San Francisco late on Sunday evening. My host insisted that we do a little sightseeing. To my surprise San Francisco was very much alive late at night. He insisted that we make a final stop at a well-known chocolate factory for a hot fudge sundae. Just what I needed to put me to sleep! On our way we passed the building of a famous mail-order catalog business.

I recognized the name because I had just ordered a pants-press from them. The object arrived promptly as advertised. In weeks an interesting process began. I began receiving, almost daily, full-color catalogs from nearly every mail-order business in the United States. My wife wanted to know why I had ordered all those catalogs. They create quite a temptation with three daughters in the house. I quickly denied guilt. "I didn't do it." We realized what had happened. The mail-order company from which I had ordered the pants-press had sold my name to other mail-order companies.

I thought about the difference between churches who prune away prospects and businesses who pay money for them. When we understand that the people on our rolls are persons for whom Jesus died, we will treasure any and every contact with them. When we prune them from our roll, we forfeit opportunities to touch their lives for the kingdom of God. Don't prune them; go find them!

At our church we tell folk there are two ways you can get off our rolls. If you join another evangelical church in our community and become active in that fellowship, we will remove your name from our roll. When you go home to be with the Lord, we will automatically remove your name. When people move from your community, you should make every attempt to help them locate a new church fellowship. Other than moving church membership, we remove people from our roll only when they go home to be with the Lord.

Yes, people occasionally want to be removed from the church roll, although they do not yet meet the prescribed conditions. Those calls or requests should be routed to the pastor. Often the individual will be going through a difficult period. He/she may want to stop receiving church mailouts or envelopes. You can readily agree to discontinue sending those items. You should, however, refuse to remove their names. Tell these persons that you care for them and that the church family cares for them. Therefore, you will retain their name in order to be available for ministry when needed. Be prepared to follow through on this commitment. You will almost always have the opportunity.

The policy of not dropping names from the roll has proved beneficial to our ministry. There have been occasions when a family has called our church during a time of bereavement. The surviving children may call, needing our help. Because the church has kept the rolls intact and maintained those names we have a new opportunity to minister to the family during a teachable moment.

On one specific occasion, we discovered two prospects for our young married department who could easily have been pruned from the roll. Our church had a bus ministry in the past. Many of those children had not attended in years. Yet their names remained on roll. With our emphasis on keeping in contact, we called the young lady. We discovered she had subsequently married and was quite interested in returning to our church.

I'm not suggesting that anyone should retain names for the sake of padding the enrollment numbers. Church growth is not about numbers, per se, but about people. I do, however, recommend that every effort be made to stay in contact with everyone God gives us in our sphere of influence. Keep the rolls intact and up to date. A name on the church or Sunday School roll is an open invitation to ministry.

The roll can be kept up to date by regular contact. A card mailed every two months or an occasional phone call can make a vast difference in the church's ministry. The person may not immediately respond, but the person making the contact receives joy and blessings that carry over to the Sunday School class and church.

Combining Classes

How often have you seen churches combine two classes to make one large one? This is a subtle way of pruning roots, but the outcome is essentially the same. The organization of the Sunday School is cut back, and this pruning process will inevitably lead to a smaller tree. Combining two classes absolves the leaders from equipping enough competent teachers, and it absolves the classes from reaching out to the community to ensure growth. Combining classes is opposite of that which needs to be done for natural growth. The healthy church will always be looking to start new units. I do not like to see classes combined even for a week or so during the summer. This inhibits natural growth and reduces the opportunities for service. Enlist a substitute and keep the class structure intact.

Cutting Back Resources and Money

Every church hits the occasional financial slump. It may occur during a building project or a down time in the local economy. When it occurs, there is a temptation to cut back in the resources available for ministry. This is a self-defeating move. Pruning the financial roots in terms of Sunday School books and the like ultimately leads to slower growth or even decline, which, in turn, creates greater financial difficulties. This is not an easy issue to resolve, but in the times of financial slowdown every effort should be given to provide the resources for growth. It may require cost cutting in other nonessential budget areas.

Tie stewardship training together with the vision for church growth and fulfilling the Great Commission. The stewardship committee must understand and be committed to church-growth principles. Pruning the financial roots greatly hampers the natural growth of the church.

Subtle Root-Pruning Techniques

A few forms of root pruning are not as obvious as those listed above. The congregation that expects the staff to do all the ministry practices root pruning. They cut back the effective caring ability of the church and thus restrict growth. The church that does not have a sufficient number of prospects has pruned the roots of opportunity. You should have one prospect for every person enrolled in the Sunday School if you are going to have sufficient roots to sustain growth.

Pruning the roots serves the bonsai well, but it hurts the growing church. God never intended for us to have cute churches. He desires for us to have healthy churches that effectively reach their communities.

Fertile Thoughts and Actions

1. What is the enrollment philosophy of your Sunday School and church? How and why are people removed from the rolls?

2. How many persons have been enrolled in your Sunday School in the past two years? How many have been unnecessarily removed through root pruning?

3. Are there ministries of your church being severely hindered by lack of funds? List these.

4. Is there a plan for increasing giving and budget that is clearly understood by the congregation.

5. What is it that you can do to help your church understand the pruning principle?

3
PINCH OFF NEW GROWTH

One of the more curious tasks the bonsai grower must do on a regular basis is to pinch off new growth. This is particularly true with little pine trees. It's quite easy to tell new growth from the old by the color alone. The new growth is light green and appears at the ends of the branches. It is a lovely, refreshing sign that the tree is healthy and growing. Thus it was difficult, to say the least, to bring myself to pinch this sure sign of new growth off my trees. But the books assured me that it was essential that this new growth be twisted off in order to keep the tree small.

You've noticed the words *pinching* and *twisted off*. This should be taken literally. The new growth is so tender, you need no tool to remove it. A simple twist is sufficient.

49

The pinching method doesn't leave the scar that pruning might.

Here once again the parallels with the church beg for comment. Most churches do not go about the task of inhibiting "new" growth in an intentional manner as I do with my bonsai, but the results are surely the same. Pinching off new members is much more subtle than pruning roots.

Pinching Off the New Members

New members join your church and they are full of excitement and joy. They are oblivious to all the flaws and imperfections of their new church home. They bask in the exhilaration of their newfound community. Now while they're still green is the time to pinch off this immature enthusiasm.

We pinch them off by refusing to allow them to become involved in the ongoing structure and life of the church. We want them to prove themselves before they are deemed worthy of service or leadership. In some churches anyone who hasn't lived in the community for twenty-five years is a newcomer. "We can't let these newcomers serve as deacons or Sunday School teachers.

We don't know what they're like." This sort of attitude pinches off new growth.

If the newcomers are new Christians, we certainly do not want to put them in places of spiritual leadership before they are prepared. This would be dangerous for them and detrimental to the life of the church. Yet we should find a place for them to exercise their spiritual gifts and to get involved. Once initial training has occurred, there are many opportunities of service open even to new Christians. Take them on visitation. Let them help plan class fellowships. Get them involved in the committee structure. Use them in the music program. *Don't pinch them off!*

In other instances those who join our churches have been growing Christians for many years. They may have moved to our community from another state and felt led to join our church. Often these folks bring in fresh ideas from their own experience. All too often churches impose some artificial waiting period that must be endured before these persons can serve in their new church home. At other times we pinch them back by turning a deaf ear to their new ideas. When we pinch back new growth, we ensure that the tree will remain small.

We pinch back new growth when we expect our new members to find a place of service without some specific plan, approach, or program for helping them. We often assume new members will find their class and their place of service on their own. The first few weeks in a new church family is a crucial time for involving new members. Follow-up must be immediate, specific, and organized or you will pinch back new growth. This is one of the most important but also most difficult tasks of the growing church. It is one thing to get members to do evangelistic outreach and quite another to get them to do adequate in-home follow-up.

Some new members have candidly told me that they felt like they were being courted when they were visiting the church. Once they joined, the only follow-up contact came in the form of offering envelopes. Now that's effectively pinching off new growth.

Pinching Off with Tradition

"We don't do things that way here!" Sounds like a refrain from a familiar hymn.

New members bring new ideas. Some may sound unorthodox. Some may be unorthodox! But *not all new ideas are bad!* One of the surest ways to pinch off new growth is to douse the enthusiasm of a new idea.

I must confess that as a pastor I am sometimes guilty of this. There are times that a layperson will come to me with a novel solution for a problem. My first reaction is to think: *What does this guy think he's doing—trying to tell me how to do my job. I'm the expert here.* We may not think in just those terms, but when we reject the new or novel suggestion out of hand we pinch off the enthusiasm of new growth. We must be open to that new idea; it may well be the moving of God's Spirit. God can, after all, speak through new ideas and new members if He so chooses.

Shut Them Out of the Class

Rarely does a group of Christians determine that they will isolate or ostracize the new member. No, it's much more subtle than that. They can do the same pinching back if they just ignore the newcomer. If newcomers to your church do not make new friends and find fellowship in the first few months, they will probably become a "backdoor" statistic. Nobody really wants it to happen. Yet we are quite ready to say: "Those newcomers just aren't committed like we are. They don't understand all the hard work we've done to build our church. They never last long around here." No wonder! It's hard to last when the attitude of the church or class is always twisting you off.

The process of shutting newcomers off from fellowship frequently occurs in churches where the adult Sunday School is not age graded. Thus there is no adult promotion and the adult classes stagnate. Newcomers threaten the "fellowship" (in truth "coziness" would be a more accurate word) of the class. They are never truly accepted into the life of that class and thus they quite expectedly "fall away."

The tragedy with the pinching off technique is that it crushes the enthusiasm of new Christians and other newcomers. Often permanent damage is done. Who has not visited that person who has been pinched off by church? They've been hurt and they're reluctant to join another church and risk being hurt again. Second, pinching off new members is often defended by a rather syrupy spirituality, "These new folks never last. They're not willing to pay their dues." I thought Christ paid all the dues. Don't we all walk on level ground at the foot of the cross? Does the Bible not teach that the last shall be first?

Ignoring Friends

We frequently pinch back evangelistic growth opportunities when we fail to ask new Christians to identify other non-Christian family members and friends who are unsaved. When people find Christ, they are usually enthusiastic to share their new-found relationship with others. These new Christians are unsure and ill-equipped to share their faith with an unsaved friend.

We must give encouragement by offering to go with them to visit the friend or family member. Send someone who can present the gospel and ask the new Christians to share their own personal testimony. This must be done immediately since new Christians will frequently forfeit these friendships soon after conversion. Their "old friends" are often dismayed that their "former" friends no longer want to do the same things they used to do together. Yet the difference in interest and life-style can provide an effective illustration for sharing the gospel.

Restrictive Enrollment

Some churches insist that people prove themselves before they can be enrolled in the Sunday School or small group organization of the church. "You must attend three times to be a member here." The intentions may be well meant, but the effect is often detrimental to evangelistic growth. The growing church will practice an open enrollment policy. This does not mean that you should lower the standards for becoming a part of your church. (The only biblical standard for church membership is a born-again relationship with Christ.) Yet there should be a small-group organization in your church that people are encouraged to join without any restriction. People enrolled and nurtured through small-group Bible study units will frequently accept Christ within the first year. Don't pinch away those fragile shoots.

Pinching Back Through Lack of Affirmation

A lack of affirmation and encouragement of both new and present members pinches back new spiritual growth. Recognize and acknowledge those spiritual breakthroughs in life. The church often expects a great deal in terms of service and giving without providing the "thank you" and biblical affirmation which must occur to ensure that new growth remains. Every healthy church needs both formal and informal methods of affirming new members and the new spiritual growth of all church members.

Some of the most neglected phrases in the church today are: Thank you; I appreciate you; Good job; We care; You are loved; How are you doing? and, May I help? These questions and affirmations must be genuine and heartfelt. They must be a constant if we are to ensure that new growth is not pinched off by discouragement and disillusionment.

The green growth at the end of the limb is the sign of life. Don't pinch it back.

Fertile Thoughts and Actions

1. What is the unwritten requirement for new members before they are asked to serve in your congregation?

2. List some traditions that keep your church from growing and reaching its full potential.

3. How healthy is the friendship network in your church? Take a brief survey of members to find out.

4. What program do you have for involving and training new members?

4

Soil Is Basic

Soil may well be the most critical element in growing a bonsai tree. The small pot contains little soil. The roots must be able to get sufficient moisture, but if the soil doesn't drain well, the roots will rot. You can buy premixed bonsai soil from most nurseries, or you can make your own. To make your own you mix sand, peat moss, and earth in equal proportions. Mix all these ingredients together using a shovel or garden trowel, depending on the amount needed. Since each tree receives only a small quantity of soil, it is important not to have chunks of clay or rock. Some bonsai trees—conifers, for example—do better in slightly drier soil. For those trees you should add two parts sand. This will allow for faster drainage. For broad-leaved trees you can use two parts earth which will retain water longer. As you learn more about bonsai, you come to understand the complexities of soil textures.

In our comparison of the church and the bonsai, what can we learn from the soil?

Understanding the Soil

The bonsai pot contains a small amount of soil, and because the soil is essential to healthy growth, a knowledge of the soil is critical. Many churches fail to grow because they do not understand the nature of the soil in their community. You will remember that the Lord taught the disciples about the importance of understanding the soil when they witnessed. Some soil is more receptive to the seed of the gospel than other forms of soil. Nonetheless, the faithful planter must continue to sow. We must never let the soil become an excuse for the bonsai condition of our church. With the aid of the Holy Spirit we can change the soil, but before we can change it we must first understand it.

What do you know about your soil? What do you know about your church community? Church members and pastors alike are often surprised to discover how little they do know. Give yourself a simple test.

1. What is the population of your community?

2. What are the age breakdowns within that population?

3. How many students attend the local elementary school(s)? How many in the high school(s)?

4. What special needs exist in your neighborhood? (Handicapped persons, hearing impaired, and so forth).

How well did you do?

Taking a Soil Sample

As you can see from our little test, the first essential bit of information is basic demographic facts. Who lives in our church community? How old are they? What is their educational background? What physical and emotional needs do they have? For example, an aging community will require more first-floor space and handicapped facilities for senior adults. A community with a high concentration of young adults will require adequate facilities for preschool and school-age children.

The answer to these and other questions should determine the organizational structure of your church as well as the allocation and use of space. These facts should help you decide what additional staffing and programming you need to add in order to meet the needs of your community. Many churches do not take a soil sample in order to determine their outreach approach to their community. Since the soil and the tree must be compatible, a failure to understand our soil will almost assuredly cause the church to remain in a bonsai condition, or worse yet, to die.

If you are wondering how to get started in collecting a soil sample, let me make a few suggestions. A first step might be a simple walk-through or drive-through survey of your community. Much can be determined by careful observation. Look for telltale clues such as swing sets, bikes, or handicapped ramps to alert you to the makeup of your community.

Much of the demographic information is available through your local government. A little work at the courthouse or library should yield good results. Call your local city or county information center to inquire about additional information concerning your community. Southern Baptist churches can request help in determining their soil condition from the Sunday School Board. The Great Commission Sunday School Program is designed to help churches understand and minister to their community. No doubt other denominations offer similar help to their churches. Just ask.

One of the most effective, but often overlooked, methods of determining soil condition is a door-to-door "needs" survey. I know that many brave souls have had their knees turn to jelly at the mere mention of door-to-door survey. The "needs" survey is different. The singular objective of this survey is to discover the real and felt needs of your community. This is much less threatening to the participant than the survey that asks about church attendance or religious preference. In the "needs" survey you will want to obtain certain basic information such as the number of children at home and their age. Beyond that, you want to discover needs.

For example, is there a need for weekday child care? In an older community, a need might exist for a day-care center for home-bound adults. You can use a simple one-question survey—"What need or needs exist in our community that you would like to see our church address?" You may have to give a few examples such as those above to prime the pump. You could also design a needs questionnaire based on the information you have already gathered and conclude it with the open-ended question mentioned above. People generally respond positively when they sense that someone is actually interested in listening to their ideas and meeting their needs.

Take the results of this information and begin to look at your program, facility, staff assignments, Bible study organization, and the like. Determine what you must do to meet the needs of the community. Be selective, no church can meet all of these needs. Move in the direction where you feel the strongest leading of the Lord. You will soon see results if you find a need and meet it.

The soil condition not only determines the kind of tree you can grow but, to some extent, the size of the tree. If the population of your community is 4,000, a megachurch model will only frustrate your people. You must establish ministry and growth goals that are realistic, given your soil conditions. Look for a role model among churches that are growing in soil conditions similar to your own. Learn from them. Study their programs and their organizational structure. Once again, I would remind you that we should never use the soil conditions as an excuse for our own lack of willingness to work at church growth. You can grow a church in any soil. You must first understand the soil and then plant the kind of church that will grow best in those conditions. The success of a church is not determined solely by its enrollment or attendance, but by its size and ministry relative to its given opportunity. True size is measured by the vision and heart to reach its local community.

A Look at Your Own Soil

Occasionally churches will go through the process of looking at their community and then fail to look at the soil in their own pot. What is the makeup of the soil in your church? Some of the obvious questions are easy to answer, but frequently are overlooked. What are the characteristics of your congregation in terms of age, educational level, racial mix, and so forth. These figures should then be compared with those discovered while studying your community. How do they correlate? What areas of opportunity have you overlooked? What must be done to reach those persons?

Let's look at an example. What if you discovered that your community had a growing population of young couples but your church was composed primarily of older adults? With these facts in hand you should see an opportunity to grow a young adult department. What then must you do? You must first develop classes for young adults or expand those you already have. You may need to allocate building space for preschool rooms. These rooms should be fresh, clean, and well-equipped. Young couples do bring preschoolers, and they are looking for a quality preschool program. Now develop a strategy for reaching the young couples. What do young couples enjoy doing? What events can we sponsor that will attract these young adults? I think you can see how to proceed.

In determining your own soil condition

you should go a step further by asking the simple question: "Who are we?" When I interviewed with the pulpit committee from First Baptist, Norfolk, I asked them that question.

One person responded: "We're not the rock church!"

I mused, "That's interesting, I wonder what material was used in building the church. Brick? Siding? Wood?" I soon discovered that he wasn't referring to building material. He was talking about a particular style of worship. The Rock Church is a large church in our community with a charismatic worship style. This man was trying to tell me that First Baptist was not charismatic in worship style or theology.

Another person responded, "We're not a typical First Church."

Once again I was curious. What is a typical First Church? For some that may imply liberal, rich, or exclusive. For others it may mean evangelistic, warm, or growing. It all depends on one's perspective and background.

I decided to rephrase my question. "If I were to visit your church and you were to visit me, what would you tell me about your church to encourage me to join you?" Lights went on! One man responded that he would tell me that the church had a strong Bible-teaching program. Another added that he would tell me about the warm family atmosphere that pervaded the whole church body. Without realizing it, they had told me something about their soil. It was a fertile soil for Bible teaching and fellowship. I affirmed them in this and said, "Now we must tell the community who we are." It is more important to tell who we are than who we are not. What is your soil like? What do you do well? Does your community know that? How can you tell them?

When examining your soil, I recommend another more penetrating step. You should look for soil conditions that stifle growth and those which could be hazardous to the life of the church. The bonsai tree will not survive long without water. Dry soil is deadly to the life of the church. Dry soil comes from a lack of prayer and commitment and is manifested in a lack of joy, enthusiasm, and vision. Complacency sets in and people no longer expect the church to grow and reach the community for Christ. Worship and Sunday School attendance become a duty. The people lose their excitement for inviting their friends to attend with them. The church withers in such dry soil.

Interestingly, a tree can survive dry soil longer than expected. Recently one of my prized bonsai trees was missed in the regular watering cycle for nearly a week. We had brought the tree indoors to decorate for a fellowship meeting, and had forgotten it. When I discovered it, I was horrified. It had dropped its blossoms and the leaves had become brittle and dry. I was sure that it was dead. With my pruning tool, I trimmed one of the branches and found that it was still green and pliable below the bark. It was still alive! I put it outside and watered and fertilized it faithfully. In two weeks the brittle leaves fell off and once again I thought all was lost. Yet I refused to give up and continued the watering and fertilizing. After several more weeks passed, I noticed that small light green leaf buds began to appear on a single branch. It was not long until the entire branch structure was covered with new leaves. The tree had missed a flowering season, but it had survived. Now it is healthy once again.

When a church allows its soil to dry out, it fails to bloom or put on fruit, but it can survive the drought. Perhaps the soil in your church has become dry. Growth has ceased and discouragement has set in. Your church need not die from the dry soil. Get on your knees together and ask God for a fresh anointing from His Spirit. Open God's Word and allow it to open you to His searchlight. Confess any and all sins He brings to your mind, turn from these, and make a renewed commitment to be the church. Dry soil can only be changed by the Father.

One other soil condition is hazardous to the health of the bonsai. Soggy soil! Soggy soil will rot the root structure of the tree and soon the blossoms and leaves will fall. Soggy soil conditions are produced when the church becomes introverted, focusing on its own needs, rather than fulfilling the Great Commission.

Root-rotting, soggy soil often occurs in the Sunday School organization when a church fails to promote adults and to create new units for growth. Churches often excuse the failure to promote and create new units because of room constraints, convenience, the desire for intimate fellowship, and other assorted excuses. Whatever the excuse, stagnation in the small-group root structure of your church will ultimately dwarf it, or, worse yet, choke off all life.

You can also cause root rot by too much emphasis on fellowship. A church should and must provide biblical fellowship and caring. We long for fellowship. Yet many churches allow coziness and cliquishness to masquerade for fellowship. Classes will often refuse to reach out to visitors, promote students, or create new units because they don't want to dilute their fellowship. True fellowship can never be diluted through numerical growth. First John 1 teaches us that the conditions for meaningful fellowship are created by the sharing of the gospel. When a small group refuses to reach out to new persons because of the "wonderful fellowship" in their class, they are fooling themselves. They may have a close-knit clique, but they do not have meaningful fellowship. Run a little test case. Send a newcomer into that class for several weeks and then ask the visitor to judge the warmth of the fellowship of that class. They'll often report that they felt excluded by the class. That's not fellowship! An overemphasis on "fellowship" will rot the roots.

An exaggerated emphasis on "quality" or "in-depth" Bible study can cause soggy soil. Often the request for in-depth Bible study thinly covers an exaggerated and arrogant spirituality. "We're so spiritual and deep that we need a separate Bible study." Then we hear the common refrain; "Those visitors just weren't serious about in-depth Bible study." Quality Bible study does not have to be obscure or exclusive. Jesus was a pretty deep teacher, but children, sinners, and other common folk found His teaching to be winsome. We must teach the Bible to win the lost and nurture the saints without excluding anyone. An exaggerated, proud emphasis on "in-depth" Bible study can choke out healthy growth.

Another condition that often creates soggy soil is the realization of the original dream. While you're scratching your head in confusion, let me illustrate. A mission church is planted with the dream that it will be self-supporting once they reach one hundred in Sunday School and have a sound financial base. Soon the big day arrives and the mission constitutes and calls their first full-time pastor. The church breathes a sigh of relief because the original dream has been accomplished. Later we look at that once rapidly growing mission and notice that it has stopped growing. They still have about one hundred in Sunday School three years later. Why did the mission fail to continue its rapid growth curve? They failed to dream a new dream.

This factor can affect churches of all sizes. Recently we finished our fourth and apparently final building program at First Baptist, Norfolk. I say "apparently final" because we have saturated our existing property and no other land appears readily available. Yet we never know what God has in store. After the first three building programs, we always had an immediate and obvious growth spurt. In each of these programs we built one phase of a master plan. In the last program we completed construction of the entire master plan. We nearly doubled our floor space in that one project, but to our surprise, no spurt of growth followed. On the contrary, the church actually settled back slightly in Sunday School attendance. Other pastors had warned me concerning the post-building blues, but I didn't listen because it had never affected us before.

Why the lull this time? What was different? In this phase we completed everything we had on the drawing board. The dream had been realized. We had arrived! Now we could relax. Before we saw any renewed signs of growth we had to dream a new dream. We had to renew the vision to reach people for Christ. We had to answer the question: "Where do we go from here?"

Changing Our Soil Condition

It's one thing to identify our soil condition, but quite another to change it. I've already indicated that dry soil can only be changed by God's Spirit as we get in the Word and on our knees. With the aid of the Holy Spirit, we can take several practical steps to change the soggy soil conditions which threaten to rot the root structure of our church.

Start by age-grading your entire Sunday School or small group structure. Promote in your adult classes each year. This keeps a healthy flow in the Sunday School structure and defeats stagnation. Start a few new units. Nothing grows like new shoots. Help your people to understand the practical reasons for promotion and creating new units.[1] Work together patiently and lovingly to accomplish these tasks. Change is always difficult and often painful.

Begin to reach out to unchurched and unsaved persons in your community. Nothing creates excitement in the church like new persons becoming involved. Put these new persons to work as soon as they are spiritually capable of serving. New people bring new ideas and they tend to break up the soggy condition of our soil.

You will need to work continually on attitudes and relationships within the church if you are to be successful in creating a good soil condition for healthy church growth. You need to face and correct negative attitudes such as those expressed in statements like: "Those newcomers are taking over our church," "Who do they think they are, we've worked and slaved for our church," and "The pastor just doesn't care about our needs, all he cares about is getting new members." These attitudes can be combated by creating an atmosphere where the interpersonal relationships within the church are healthy. God's people need to learn to love one another. Paul gave good advice for our relationships in Philippians 2:3-5:

> Do nothing from selfishness or empty conceit, but with humility of mind let each of you regard one another as more important than himself; do not merely look out for your own personal interests, but also for the interests of others. Have this attitude in yourselves which was in Christ Jesus.

Your church will grow if you ensure that the soil is healthy.

Fertile Thoughts and Ideas

1. Take a close look at your community. Using the questions on p. 63 as a starting point, what did you learn about soil?

2. In light of what you learned, what is your church doing right?

3. What changes need to be made in your soil conditions?

4. What are you willing to do personally to facilitate these changes?

5. Do you see signs of soggy or dry soil? What can be done to change these conditions?

Note

1. Several of the books listed in the final chapter will help you to learn and communicate concerning basic church growth principles.

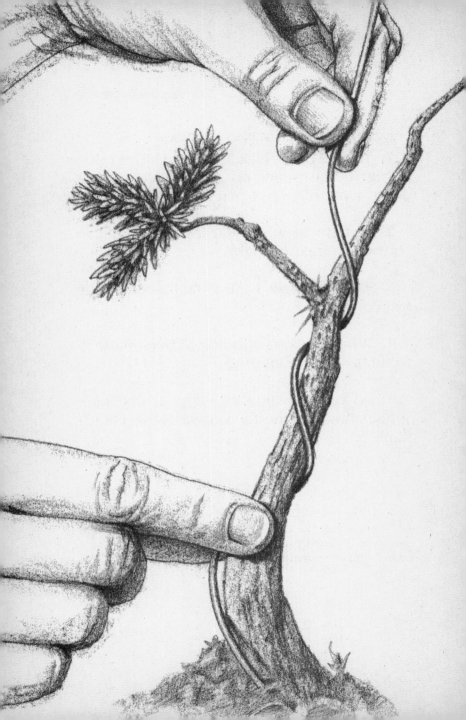

5

CREATING AGE AND DIRECTION

One of the most interesting techniques of the art of bonsai is that of creating the appearance of age and forcing the direction of growth. By stripping the bark from a particular limb, a tree can be made to look more ancient than it is. This illusion of age is intended to make the miniature tree look even more like its mature counterpart in nature. On a trip to Florida I recently purchased such a tree. Upon returning I proudly displayed it for my daughters. They liked the tree which appeared to be growing out of a rock but they wanted me to cut off the dead limbs. "It makes it look like it's dying," they noted.

A second technique of mimicking the process of nature is to force the direction of growth by the use of wires. If you ever observe a collection of bonsai trees you will no doubt notice that many of the limbs have been wrapped with copper wires. These wires force the tree to grow in a certain direction and configuration. A tree can be wired in such a way that it appears as if it has been windblown for years. It looks convincing, but it's all an illusion.

The Illusion of Fellowship

Many churches stay small because they have artificially created the illusion of fellowship. Some small groups have become introverted and their coziness bears a striking resemblance to authentic fellowship, but it's not the same. True biblical fellowship is created by the sharing of the gospel. Fellowship is ultimately a *by-product* of sharing the good news.

One of the greatest biblical passages on fellowship is found in 1 John 1. John wrote that we (believers) declare the things which we have seen, heard, and experienced that others may have fellowship with us and our fellowship is with the Father. Christian fellowship is both human and divine. Fellowship is *with God* and it is *with us*. True biblical fellowship must have both vertical and horizontal dimensions. John's concern was that unbelievers would experience Christian joy and consequently that the joy of believers would be full. Notice that our joy is actually made complete as we share the gospel. We do not lose fellowship when we add new members to our group. True fellowship can never be diluted by numbers, only by complacency and sin.

Many churches remain artificially small under the guise that growth would dissipate fellowship. I think for some there is a genuine fear that natural growth will destroy the warmth they have come to treasure. For others it is simply a selfish way of guarding their own personal interests. Many classes become cliques that have their own agenda and the newcomer is clearly made to feel unwelcome. These groups are usually reluctant to promote members to the correct age groups or to help start new units. They rarely encourage their members to leave the class and serve elsewhere within the church family.

We often associate fellowship with cookouts, potluck meals, party times or coffee and donuts before class. These events are important; adults need and desire to belong to a group. But biblical fellowship is much more than a list of class activities. Biblical fellowship demands interpersonal relationships where we can drop the mask we so often wear. Paul gave a graphic description of fellowship in 1 Corinthians 12:25-27;

> that there should be no division in the body, but that the members should have the same care for one another. And if one member suffers, all the members suffer with it; if one member is honored, all the members rejoice with it. Now you are Christ's body, and individually members of it.

A speaker at the Ridgecrest Conference Center near Asheville, North Carolina, once illustrated fellowship in action in a small group. This incident occurred in an adult Sunday School class composed mainly of young professionals—attorneys, physicians, C.P.A.s, and businessmen. The teacher committed the cardinal teaching "sin." He asked a relatively new member to read aloud the

Scripture passage for that morning's lesson. The new member was either poorly educated or a poor reader. He had great difficulty reading aloud and stumbled on a number of words. The teacher thought he was having trouble pronouncing some of the words because he was reading from the *King James Version* and asked, "What translation are you reading?" The newcomer closed his Bible, looked at the cover, which had the word *concordance* written just below *Holy Bible*, and thoughtfully replied, "the Concordance Version." Not one of the highly educated members laughed or even smiled. That was fellowship.

Recently our church fellowship has been tested as many of our men and a few of our women have been called overseas because of the conflict in the Middle East. The Sunday School classes and the entire church family responded with incredible speed. Care letters and cards have been written, support groups formed, and offers of assistance such as baby-sitting have been abundant.

Fellowship does not occur simply because we have a room in our building dedicated to potluck dinners; fellowship occurs only when the interpersonal relationships in the church are kept healthy.

Many classes have stripped the bark from the limb of their classes and they give an appearance of having fellowship, but they're not truly open to new folk. They're not interested in getting involved in their lives and hurting or rejoicing with them. In the church we're not after the appearance of fellowship, we're after the reality.

Sharing Authority

Christians often have an illusion of openness to new members only to slam the door when it appears that the newcomer may be gaining authority. Some people fear church growth because they enjoy being the big fish in a small pond. They really don't want to share their power. They give the illusion that they want help, but when their authority is threatened they often strike out in such a way that the new member is made to feel unwanted.

Forcing the Direction

Many churches fail to grow to maturity because they artificially force the church in a particular direction. The largest copper wire in our arsenal is that of tradition. When it's wrapped around the tree it says: "We've never done it that way," or perhaps "We've tried that before," or "It won't work here." We fear new ideas. We're afraid to try new things, to allow the Spirit to direct our growth. Since church growth is supernatural, we must be willing to allow the wind of the Spirit to move us as He wills. We cannot allow our traditions and our comfort zones to wire us into preset patterns.

A second wire is altogether different. We can artificially force the direction of our church by modeling one church after another without due consideration to the distinctives of a particular situation. We can and must learn from other growing churches, but we cannot wire our church to be just like them.

I learned this the hard way while pastoring a small rural church in Wolf Creek, Kentucky. As soon as I arrived on the field, I started an aggressive evangelism training program. I had seen this program work well in my home church in Winston-Salem. I wanted to reach my new community and this was the only model I knew. Thus I forced my church in one direction for church growth—a direction for which they were not prepared and one which may not have been most suited to any new church field. To tell the truth, I had not spent sufficient time to discover the most suitable method for growing this church in the most efficient manner.

Another wire we use to force the direction of our church is the wire of comfort. "We like things the way they are. We're comfortable. We're making budget, paying the pastor; we get along quite well, thank you." This comfort wire can cause the church to be restrictive in its thinking. "Those folks will never fit in here."

A prominent businessman in our community joined our church. Not long afterward he attended visitation and accompanied me on a visit. As the evening progressed, the couple being visited shared their testimony and began to ask questions about the church. I answered the inquiries and began to tell them about the wonderful programs we offered. The conversation flowed freely among the four of us. The businessman who was my visitation partner sealed the visit when he told why he joined our church.

He had been visiting for several months before he decided to join. He liked the preaching, the choir, and the programs, but he just wasn't sure he wanted to join and he didn't know why. One morning at the invitation numerous people responded to join the church. Some were businessmen in nice suits, others were clean-cut young couples. Mixed in with the others was a young man with a ponytail that stretched halfway down his back. He created quite a contrast. The businessman watched and to his surprise the church accepted all with equal warmth and joy. At that moment he knew that he too must be part of a church that welcomed such variety. We refuse to force the direction of our church with any artificial means.

We need not force the direction of our church's growth, we must move at the Spirit's direction to meet the needs of our community. The perfect bonsai creates an illusion. For all intents and purposes, it looks like its counterpart which has been left to grow naturally in its proper environment.

There's one important difference: the bonsai is a decorative miniature. We have been commanded to fulfill the Great Commission, not to collect miniature churches that look like the real thing.

Fertile Thoughts and Actions

1. List situations which can create an illusion of fellowship.

2. What conveniences are keeping your Sunday School and church from growing?

3. Are there factors at work which are artificially forcing the direction of your church's growth?

6

THE DILEMMA OF THE BONSAI

The bonsai is a lovely piece of art, but it creates some unique dilemmas for the owner. Growing a bonsai in a ceramic pot can be a much more difficult task than growing a full-sized tree in its natural habitat. Did God call us to miniaturize His church, or to let Him grow it?

Cute, but Not Practical

As much as I love my collection of bonsai trees, I recognize that they do create several unique problems. First and most obvious, they are *ornamental,* but not *practical.* The little pot is lovely. The miniature tree looks like the real thing. In fact, I have a little tangerine tree that actually has tangerines. They're about the size of the tip of my thumb. They're not very edible or filling.

93

That's the dilemma. The bonsai is cute, but it does not have a great deal of practical use to anyone. It's a piece of art. It can be used to decorate one's home, but that's about all.

When we artificially create a bonsai church, we get the same results. The building may have lovely stained-glass windows. The pot that holds the church may be a work of art, but the tree in that pot is not very functional. God didn't call us to create a decorative piece of art, but a growing, living community. He called us to fulfill the Great Commission in our given area of responsibility. We cannot keep the church artificially small to satisfy our own personal desires or those of a few members. We must allow God to grow us to full maturity.

Daily Watering

The size of the pot and the limitations of the root ball require that the bonsai be watered daily. When I go away for several days I have to get a baby-sitter for my bonsai trees. My wife jokingly comments that when I go away for a pastor's conference and call home, my first question is "Did you water the bonsai?" That's not true! I'm smart enough now to ask Paula how she and the kids are before I ask about the trees. But, the fact is, my little trees require constant attention.

An artificially miniaturized church usually requires constant attention. The pastor is often called on to be a "hand holder" rather than a Great Commission growth agent to reach the community. Sometimes the quip is heard: "Our pastor doesn't care for us, all he's interested in are those prospects." Translation: "We want him to water us daily." The miniature church is actually much more demanding than is the naturally growing church. If I had taken the little pine tree I chose to bonsai and planted it in my yard, it would have taken much less daily care to grow in a natural, healthy manner.

The church that intentionally miniaturizes itself often develops a demanding attitude. Everything must be done to meet "my needs." The church exists not only to meet the spiritual needs of its members, but to reach the world for Christ.

Plucking off the Dead Needles

One of the most time-consuming tasks for the bonsai grower is the plucking of dead needles from pine trees. One of the tools in my bonsai arsenal is a pair of tweezers. To keep an evergreen bonsai healthy, the dead needles must be plucked from the tree. The miniature evergreen doesn't have the advantage of the forces of nature which would naturally discard the needles if the tree were of normal size. On a regular schedule I sit down at the table and pluck tiny needles one by one from my evergreens.

The miniaturized church demands constant needle-plucking. It rarely is exposed to the forces of its own community. It is pampered and coddled with everything being done for it. Most of the money is spent on self-esteem items such as the pot or decorative items to showcase the pot. The members are called upon to do very little to ensure the healthy growth of their own church. Truthfully, the miniature church expects the pastor to pull away all the dead needles that could afflict them. He becomes the hired gardener of the church whose only function is to take care of "us." This will soon destroy the pastor's heart for evangelism and ultimately cripple his ministry. It will cause the church to lose its passion for soul winning and become a miniaturized display model of the real thing.

The Demand for a Greenhouse

No doubt you've already concluded that bonsai demand rather specialized care. This can be especially true during the winter. Since a bonsai is a *real* tree, it must experience the seasons which are natural to its annual development. I learned this the hard way when I kept a pine tree in my office throughout the entire year. It died, I was told, because it didn't experience the normal winter dormancy. Thus a bonsai must have a winter rest, but it can't endure severe weather conditions. Its root depth is so shallow in the small container that it will easily freeze to death. This means that the bonsai demands a greenhouse for winter survival.

The church that has been kept artificially small frequently demands very specialized care. It is often controlled by one or two large family groups, and if the environment is not carefully controlled, major problems can occur and premature death can result. Churches are often "bonsaied" by families who have enjoyed exercising control by their money or influence in the community. They like the church the way it is! They're quite comfortable and well they should be—they run the church. When potential growth threatens their dominance, conditions can become quite hostile for the pastor or other newcomers.

God did not create the church for our pleasure or our control. It was not fashioned to make us comfortable. The church was created as the showplace of God's manifold wisdom (see Eph. 3:10). It was created to be His messianic community, extending the plan of redemption to the world (see Matt. 16:18). It was called to carry out the Great Commission (28:19-20).[1] Whose kingdom do we desire to build—our own or His?

A healthy, maturing church requires no greenhouse. It has been created by God with the resources to grow and withstand the onslaught of the adversary and the conditions of the environment. The gates of hell cannot stand against the church that is committed to *be the church*.

Fertile Thoughts and Actions

1. Are there any symptoms that indicate that your church requires daily watering?

2. What are some ways to get people out of their comfort zones?

3. List the things your congregation will be willing to do even if it is inconvenient to reach people for Christ?

Note

1. For a more detailed discussion of the nature of the New Testament church see my book: *The Official Rulebook of the New Church Game* (Nashville: Broadman Press, 1990).

7

CHURCH GROWTH IS NATURAL AND SUPERNATURAL

The church is designed to grow. Jesus told His disciples: "I will build My church" (Matt. 16:18). The scriptural images of the church imply natural, healthy growth. The church is referred to as a field, a body, and a building in progress. Paul gave eloquent expression to this natural design for growth in 1 Corinthians 3:6-9.

> I planted, Apollos watered, but *God was causing the growth*. So then neither the one who plants nor the one who waters is anything, but *God who causes the growth*. Now he who plants and he who waters are one; but each will receive his own reward according to his own labor. For we are God's fellow workers; you are God's field, God's building (italics mine).

In Ephesians 4:11-16, where Paul discussed the proper working of the gifted body, he concluded:

> but speaking the truth in love we are to *grow up in all aspects into Him,* who is the head, even Christ, from whom the whole body, being fitted and held together by that which every joint supplies, according to the proper working of each individual part, causes the growth of the body for the building up of itself in love (vv. 15-16, italics mine).

The growth of the church is both natural and supernatural. The church was designed by God to grow *naturally,* but all church growth is a *supernatural* miracle. In truth, the church will experience growth if we remove artificial and often selfish barriers we have used to keep our church artificially small—to keep it a bonsai church.

Defining the Bonsai Church

The conclusions of this study do not in any way imply that a small church is inferior to a large church. The bonsai church is a church which has been kept *artificially* small. Its natural growth has been hampered by human attempts to keep it small or inattention to the biblical pattern and methods for growth. Many methods can be used to keep a church small. Some of these bonsai techniques have been applied in ignorance of God's plan for church growth and others have been done from a selfish desire to be comfortable or control the church.

The bonsai church may be cute, but it's not practical. It is ornamental rather than fruit bearing. It is a distortion of God's original plan.

Seeking God-given Size

The healthy church will grow naturally as God gives it growth. Further, a church's growth cannot always be measured by size alone. There are many species of trees. Some trees will grow to a larger natural size than will others. The redwood and the dogwood can hardly be compared.

We live in the era of the megachurch. Great attention has been given to very large churches. They certainly play a vital role in God's work in a given community. They must not be dismissed as inauthentic or mere expressions of the pastor's ego. If they are faithful to their commission, God Himself will provide for their growth. On the other hand, not every church should or could become a megachurch. A small community cannot support megachurch growth. The resources in terms of people are simply not available.

In 1972, I pastored a church in Wolf Creek, Kentucky, where the population was about 600. Our Sunday School grew to over 100 and we baptized fifty-three persons in eighteen months. My next full-time pastorate was in Galax, Virginia. The church membership in Galax was actually larger than the entire population of Wolf Creek. In my present pastorate, the church membership is once again larger than the population of Galax. Neither Wolf Creek nor Galax could support a church of the size of First Baptist, Norfolk. Therefore church growth must be natural to the God-given size and opportunity.

It is equally true that not all areas of the same community will yield equal growth opportunities. Some churches are located in transitional neighborhoods. They feel a strong call to continue to minister to that neighbor. The soil conditions in this transitional area may not be as conducive to growth as those in a mushrooming suburban community.

There may also be different soil conditions in different areas of the country. Alabama, for example, may be more fertile than Wisconsin or Wyoming. Thus church growth must be measured according to many environmental factors. It is nonetheless essential that every church seek to fulfill the Great Commission in the context of its God-given opportunity. We must, however, be careful not to blame soil conditions for our own laziness or unwillingness to grow.

The church leadership must have a good understanding of the church's soil conditions and total environment. For example, a church in a community with many retirement-age persons needs to design programming aimed at reaching those persons. Frequently I see churches develop a certain style of music program with little consideration to the particular tastes of their community. Since music is an essential component of the growing church, the worship committee and church leaders must show sensitivity in developing a music and worship style which will reach and minister to their particular community.

Likewise, the Sunday School organization must be developed with a view to the soil conditions. A church in a community densely populated with young adults should organize a large preschool department.

Certain principles of church growth must be understood and utilized by every church.[1] There are many methods of applying these principles. Methodology may vary from situation to situation. The wise leader will utilize growth principles and discover those methods that work best in local soil conditions.

When a Tree Outgrows Its Pot

What do I do when a tree outgrows its pot? This is one of the most frequent questions I hear and rightly so since the pot is probably the most restricting element to natural growth. Some of the pots mentioned in this book can be easily replaced. If the church's vision is the restricting pot, pastor and lay leaders can often find a greater vision by attending a growth conference or denominational training center. Another method is to visit a church with a similar soil condition that is showing healthy growth. We must learn from one another. Church growth is not a competitive sport but a cooperative kingdom activity.

The pots of leadership and organization naturally go together. Ongoing leadership training is essential to the life of any healthy church. The expanding organization requires a sufficient number of well-trained leaders. The equipping of the laity for ministry appears to me to be the primary role of the pastor/staff.

The most confining pot is that of land and building space. Short of new construction, space can be attained by multiple use of the same facilities. We may have to think outside the lines. The church is not restricted to Sunday morning at 11:00 for worship. Multiple use of the building is good stewardship because it provides virtually free space. Off-site space can often be found. The building of adequate space is a more normal solution to the space problem.

Land is a little more tricky. Dual Sunday Schools, for example, will provide additional building space, but will in turn put even greater stress on available parking spaces. Parking decks have proved to be too costly for all but a few churches. Off-site parking is an option. A few churches have successfully used a park-and-ride system with a shuttle service. But it appears that most American church members are presently unwilling to make the sacrifice necessary to put up with this inconvenience. We are spoiled!

Some churches have solved the land problem by relocating. This is certainly *one* choice and may be the wisest choice in many situations. The church that relocates must ensure that the community being left will still be reached by an evangelical witness. Relocating is not the only solution. Many churches have decided that they will continue to growth through the planting of new churches in other areas of their community. Here, care should be taken to plant a healthy church that is committed to natural biblical growth.[2] This church should be one that is suited to its new soil conditions. Church planting is a healthy method of church growth.

Growing in All Aspects

In Ephesians 4:15 Paul wrote that the church should grow *in all aspects* into Christ. Most church growth books point out the difference between biological, transfer, and evangelistic growth. Biological growth comes from within. The church experiences this growth when it baptizes the children and youth of its own members. This is valid growth and every church should seek to reach its own. Transfer growth occurs when individuals transfer their membership from another church, either from outside the present community or within. This too is valid church growth, but must not be allowed to degenerate into sheep stealing. These two forms of numerical growth should not be the only form of church growth.

Every church must be involved in evangelistic growth. Somewhere the idea has crept in that some churches are not called to have an evangelistic ministry. We must recognize that there is a natural variety among churches even as there is variety in the trees of nature. Yet the church, by definition, must be evangelistic. The church cannot fulfill the Great Commission without an evangelistic outreach to its community. *Evangelistic growth is natural to every church.*

Beyond these three forms of numerical growth, there are other forms of growth. There must be growth in biblical knowledge and moral standards. Churches must grow through the development of Christian character in their membership. There is growth which issues in greater mission awareness and stewardship. This will often lead to mission involvement both in and beyond one's community. I have already mentioned growth through the planting of new churches as an authentic form of church growth. As you can see, not all church growth is numerical growth. Yet, I must again add a word of caution. Numerical growth should not be discounted or ignored. Churches often avoid the matter of numerical growth by arguing that they emphasize other forms of growth. Church growth is not either/or but both/and. Avoiding the topic of numerical growth is often a defense mechanism for laziness, lack of commitment, or desire to remain comfortably small. It is one of the leading causes of bonsai churches.

God desires to build your church. This doesn't necessarily mean it will become a megachurch. It does mean that your church must grow to take full advantage of its God-given opportunities. Arthur Flake wrote:

> There is inspiration in numbers, but let it be understood that a school does not necessarily have to have an enrollment of 1,000 members to be a great school. It may be a really great school and have an attendance of a hundred or even less. However, no Sunday School is worthy of being called a great school unless it is reaching a large majority of the people who should attend it. This is true no matter what other claims to efficiency it may have.[3]

What Flake said in 1922 concerning the Sunday School is equally true today. Your church is responsible for reaching a large majority of those who should attend. *Your church can grow!*

Fertile Thoughts and Actions

1. Briefly describe your understanding of the biblical model of church growth using the Scriptures mentioned in this chapter.

2. What soil conditions are affecting your church's ability to grow?

3. What are the factors in your worship services that are affecting your ability to grow?

4. Is there a particular age group in your community that your church should be providing ministries for which it currently is not providing?

5. List the available opportunities to provide additional space and land around your church's facilities. Should your church consider relocating in order to fulfill God's challenge for your church's ministry?

6. How evangelistic is your Sunday School and church? What can be done to improve the evangelistic climate of your Sunday

School and church? List some practical steps that you are willing to do to see that this is accomplished.

Notes

1. Ken Hemphill and R. Wayne Jones, *Growing an Evangelistic Sunday School* (Nashville: Broadman Press, 1989), chapter 4.

2. Jack Redford, *Planting New Churches* (Nashville: Broadman Press, 1978).

3. Arthur Flake, *Building a Standard Sunday School* (Nashville: The Sunday School Board, 1922), 28.

8

GROWING A
NATURAL TREE

What do I do now? How do I get started growing a healthy natural tree? Perhaps these questions have entered your mind as you have read this book.

Congratulations

Congratulations! You have already made a valuable beginning. Reading this book indicates both your interest in church growth and your willingness to learn how to grow your church. You have already started dealing with the pot of limited vision. Now you need to communicate this vision to others in your church.

If you are a layperson, you will want to begin with your pastor. Share this book with him or give him a copy that he can read and mark. Ask him if you can discuss these concepts with him after he has completed the book. Pray for him while he is reading the book. The pastor is called by God to lead the church; therefore, it is essential that he share the vision for church growth. It has been my experience that a majority of pastors want to see their church grow. He will be delighted to have your encouragement. If he is somewhat reluctant to move ahead, be patient and allow God to bring conviction to this area.

If you are a pastor, you will need to communicate these ideas to your congregation. God has called you to provide the leadership for your congregation. This will give you an excellent opportunity to provide that visionary leadership. I have found that most laypersons want to see their church grow once they understand the principles of church growth. Laypersons often fear that which they do not understand. The more that you can do in the way of communication, the better. You could use this book or other church-growth books as a study course. Encourage open discussion and saturate the group time with prayer. I would encourage you to begin this process with those who have been elected to leadership positions by the church. If these trusted laypersons adopt these growth ideas, they can help you communicate them effectively to the rest of the congregation.

Above all, be patient and prayerful. These ideas may meet with some resistance in the beginning simply because they are new. Ask God to make their hearts receptive.

Keep Growing

This book, by design, only introduces the topic of church growth. The more you can read, the better prepared you will be to lead your church to grow. You will find any number of fine books on church growth at your local Christian book store. To help you begin your library, I have listed and summarized a few books. This is a very partial list but you will find additional resources by reading these books. I have paid particular attention to those books which emphasize church growth through the Sunday School/small-group structure of the church. I do this from a personal bias. I believe that the best way to grow a church is through an evangelistic Sunday School.

Growing an Evangelistic Sunday School, Ken Hemphill and Wayne Jones, Broadman Press, 1989. This book compares church growth thinking with basic Sunday School work and deals with theory and practice. The Sunday School can function as an integrated church-growth tool when it has a clear focus on evangelism.

Growing and Winning Through the Sunday School, ed., Harry Piland, Convention Press, 1981. This is a basic but critical book. It is a "how-to" book on Sunday School growth.

Total Church Life, Darrell W. Robinson, Broadman Press, 1985. Robinson's plan for church growth revolves around three major points of strategy: Exalt the Savior, Equip the Saints, and Evangelize the Sinner. This book is aimed primarily at the church staff.

The Nuts and Bolts of Church Growth, Paul Powell, Broadman Press, 1982. Here is a book full of practical ideas by a man who made them work in his own church.

Your Church Can Grow, C. Peter Wagner, Regal Books, 1984. This one is a classic, but never outdated. Wagner describes seven vital signs of a healthy church. Give your church a spiritual checkup.

Leading Your Church to Grow, C. Peter Wagner, Regal Books, 1984. This book is addressed to both pastor and congregation. For this reason it is an ideal resource for imparting vision and goal ownership. Study this book with your congregation.

Balanced Church Growth, Ebbie Smith, Broadman Press, 1984. A clear introduction to church growth.

Attend a Church-growth Conference

Church growth and Sunday School conferences are held in nearly every area of our country. You can find one near you. Begin with denominational resources. They are usually less expensive than those sponsored by various churches or growth organizations. Often they will be tailored to the specific needs of your church. I have benefitted greatly from Sunday School conferences provided by our state and national conventions. Do not, however, avoid other conferences simply because of the cost. They are a good investment in your ministry and your church's work. Participating in a growth conference allows you to interact with others who have experienced similar problems that you are facing. The conference also provides a contagious spirit of excitement that you cannot catch from reading a book.

Talk to Those Who Have Done It

Church growth is not a competitive sport but a team effort. When you discover another church that is doing a good job at reaching its community for Christ, set up an appointment to talk to the pastor or staff. I can tell you from experience that they will be delighted to share any lessons they have learned. I have gained greatly from talking to those who have done it. In turn, I and my staff have had the great joy to share our story with many pastors and staff. Those who are committed to church-growth principles in their own church want to see your church grow, too. Don't hesitate to ask for help.

Make a Commitment to Biblical Growth

Church growth is natural but not easy. It is a lifelong process that requires continual planning, implementation, and plain hard work. It is worth it because church growth enables the church to fulfill the Great Commission. If you're going to stay with growth principles during the difficult times you must make a commitment to be a church-growth agent. The biblical images concerning the church imply growth. The Great Commission mandates that the church reach those who are unsaved. This will provide natural, healthy church growth. Don't be discouraged if your church doesn't explode overnight. Be patient! Growth principles work, but they may take time. The soil where the church is planted may not yet be receptive to the gospel. Use your Sunday School or small group structure to focus on evangelism. Remember, prayer is the key to changing the receptivity of the soil.

Look at Your Pots

If, through reading this book, you have discovered some "small pots" that are constricting the growth of your church, begin now to take the steps to resolve your problem. If you need building space immediately, consider multiple Sunday Schools. An excellent guide for establishing multiple Sunday Schools is available free from the Baptist Sunday School Board in Nashville, Tennessee. The use of multiple Sunday Schools will provide additional time to begin the building planning process.

You must enlarge the Sunday School organization and leadership first if you intend for your church to grow. I recommend age grading your Sunday School. This will enable the visitors to your Sunday School to readily identify their class. Age grading also provides the most natural method of enlarging the Sunday School organization. For example, you may begin with an adult Sunday School class for those twenty to twenty-nine years of age. When the enrollment of this class exceeds thirty you could start a new teaching unit by dividing the class into two classes. One could be for those twenty to twenty-four and the other for those twenty-five to twenty-nine. This will help you to expand your organization and maintain the integrity of your grading system. The age-grading system also recognizes the common needs that are shared by those of similar age and life setting.

You cannot enlarge the organization without enlarging your pool of leadership. Leadership enlistment and training is a never-ending task of the growing church. Use variety and creativity in the solicitation of leaders. The best method of leadership recruitment is one on one. Most listeners think that the announcements from the pulpit are intended for someone other than themselves. Leaders must be prayerfully approached on an individual basis. Ask God to lead you to the right persons for leadership training. Pray that God will prepare their hearts before you approach them. Ask them to pray about the opportunity for service in a particular area. Assure them that the church will provide adequate training. Set a date to get back together to discuss their decision for service.

A good source for discovering potential leaders are those presently serving as leaders. Encourage your teachers to help you recruit other leaders. This process will not work unless your existing leaders are committed to church growth through the Sunday School. If they see their class as their personal property, they will be reluctant to encourage class members to serve in other positions. It is important that the lay leaders of the church have a Great-Commission consciousness. I think it would be a good plan to ask your teachers to attempt to recruit another person to work as their aid with a view to full-time service. Various evangelism tools such as Evangelism Explosion and Continuous Witness Training have used this methodology with good success. Each participant is expected to recruit two persons to be their trainees. Why wouldn't this concept work with Sunday School? Ask each Sunday School leader to recruit one additional person who could teach in their age division. They could then invite them to sit in on the class for a few weeks as an observer.

You must provide adequate training if you are going to have a growing Sunday School. Today's fast-paced environment requires that the church use a variety of methods for teacher training. You can offer training for one night a week for eight or ten consecutive weeks. This works well for some people's schedules. You might also try a Friday night/ Saturday morning training blitz. We have discovered that many persons are more likely to give up one evening and one morning than they are to commit to extended training periods. Our minister of education recently conducted a one-night training session that he called Midnight Madness. It began at 7:00 p.m., and concluded at midnight. Over fifty persons attended.

You must be willing to do whatever is necessary to secure and train adequate leadership because this is the key to natural church growth. After the initial training, you should provide weekly training and encouragement. We call this weekly session our Sunday School Strategy Planning meeting. This meeting is essential for continued growth. Whatever the cost, the results will be well worth the sacrifice.

Nurture the Root Structure and Encourage New Growth

Simply refuse to prune the root structure of your church. When you discover inactive persons on your church or Sunday School roll, don't remove them; go get them. These persons should be first priority on your visitation list. I have discovered that many of those people who are chronically inactive in church may never have accepted Christ as their personal Savior. They may have joined the church or Sunday School without fully understanding the good news of the gospel. Don't lose your opportunity to share the gospel with these folk by tossing their name in the trash can. Others may have become inactive out of apathy or through hurt feelings. In either case these persons must be lovingly cared for by their Christian family.

Develop programs for encouraging new members. Every church, regardless of size, needs a new-member orientation class. This class can be taught by the pastor or a layperson under his supervision. This class can be a simple one-session orientation to the church, or it can be a more structured and more intensive class designed to cover such matters as church history, distinctive doctrines, membership responsibilities, ministries offered, and other such matters as deemed necessary to responsible church membership. Try to involve every new member in small-group Bible study. Members who do not get attached to a small group through the church have less connection to the church. They are easily "pinched off."

I like to invite all the new members to my home once a month for an informal fellowship time. This lets them meet me and my family and ask questions about the church. This is another way to ensure that the new growth is not pinched from the tree. Find a place of ministry involvement for new members as quickly as possible. Many churches miss golden opportunities to utilize the spiritual gifts of new members by failing to involve them in the ministries of the church quickly. New members often demonstrate greater enthusiasm for their newfound church home than do those who have been part of the church for a longer period of time. Capitalize on this natural and healthy excitement.

Ensure that all of your Sunday School classes schedule regular fellowship events. These need not be elaborate. A simple covered-dish dinner will suffice. Allow ample time for conversation and ensure that no one is excluded. These class fellowships will provide the informal time for building relationships that is often lacking on Sunday morning due to the press of time.

Focus on Evangelism

One factor that growing churches have in common is a clear focus on evangelism. The Great Commission establishes evangelism as the first priority of the church. The church that understands its primary mission in terms of this scriptural mandate will be a healthy, growing church. Focusing on evangelism will not compromise the quality of your pastoral care ministry or water down your fellowship. On the contrary, the focus on soul-winning enhances the other ministries of the church. Evangelism is the engine that drives biblical church growth.

Your Church Can Grow

God has provided all the resources necessary for balanced church growth. Your church can be an exciting part of God's plan for world redemption. Allow God to remove the restraints which have kept your church from growing naturally in a supernatural way.